Grade 5

Wake Up, Brain!!™

300 Brain-Stretching Challenges
for Language Arts, Math, Geography and More…

D1278606

Michelle Ball & Barbara Morris

ecs

These popular teacher resources and activity books are available from
ECS Learning Systems, Inc., for Grades K-6.

ECS Learning Systems, Inc.
P.O. Box 440 • Bulverde, Texas 78163-0440
Web site: www.educyberstor.com
To order, or for a complete catalog, contact the publisher or your local school supply store.

Editor: Shirley J. Durst
Cover Design and Page Layout: Anh N. Le

ISBN-10: 1-57022-228-2   ISBN-13: 978-1-57022-228-3

Copyright infringement is a violation of Federal Law.

© 2000, 2007 by ECS Learning Systems, Inc., Bulverde, Texas. All rights reserved. No part of this publication may be reproduced, translated, stored in a retrieval system, or transmitted in any way or by any means (electronic, mechanical, photocopying, recording, or otherwise) without prior written permission from ECS Learning Systems, Inc.

Photocopying of student worksheets by a classroom teacher at a non-profit school who has purchased this publication for his/her own class ispermissible. Reproduction of any part of this publication for an entire school or for a school system, by for-profit institutions and tutoring centers, or for commercial sale is strictly prohibited.

Printed in the United States of America.

Table of Contents

About this Book

All rights reserved

ECS Learning Systems, Inc.

About this Book

My inspiration for *Wake Up, Brain!!* came when I was challenged to keep track of the grammar, spelling, language, geography, and math concepts taught in my multi-age classroom. As an organizational tool, I created mini lesson plans for tracking curriculum elements for each grade or skill level. The plan included activities in five different curricular areas, plus one riddle.

My co-author, Barbara Morris, created a student- and teacher-friendly format on her computer. As time passed, we wrote more and more activities for grades 1, 2, and 3, and eventually created *Wake Up, Brain!!* for grades 4, 5, and 6, as well.

I use *Wake Up, Brain!!* as my daily mini lesson plan and expand the ideas in detail on the chalkboard or in class discussion. What a time-saver! No researching ideas or deciding what lessons to use. Students can finish all 5 activities and try to solve the riddle in as little as 5 to ten minutes.

Kids love *Wake Up, Brain!!*, too. I am constantly amazed and delighted at how practice with these mini-lessons enhances student learning in the individual subject areas. It only took a week or two for my students to get accustomed to reviewing the five subject areas at once. Now it's one of their favorite ways to learn!

Michelle Ball

ECS Learning Systems, Inc.   All rights reserved

Each book in the Wake Up, Brain!! series covers the necessary elements for teaching grammar, language, spelling, geography, and math for a specific grade level. Whether you are a teacher in a traditional or multi-age classroom, a homeschooler, or a parent wanting to become more involved in your child's school work, *Wake Up, Brain!!* is for you.

Use *Wake Up, Brain!!* for—

✦ graded daily mini-lessons

✦ teacher-led or independent practice

✦ group practice

✦ assessment of student skills, including special needs

✦ reinforcement of essential concepts

✦ homework, extra credit, or quizzes

✦ acquainting parents with the basic curriculum

All rights reserved   ECS Learning Systems, Inc.

Wake Up, Brain!!

Name: _____

Grammar

1. would you be surprised if i didnt talk for too hours

_____

_____

2. karen asked you to call her before 730 did you

_____

_____

Spelling

3. Put these words in alphabetical order.

| stop | little | house | know | be | ride |

_____   _____

_____   _____

_____   _____

Language

4. Number these sentences in the right order.

#	He liked it and started making it to sell.
#	Thomas Adams was an inventor.
#	In a few years he owned a chewing gum factory.
#	He tried chewing "chicle" from a tree in Mexico.

ECS Learning Systems, Inc.   All rights reserved

Wake Up, Brain!!

Name: _____

Geography

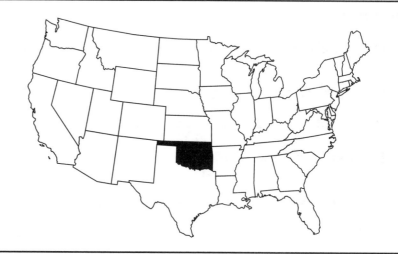

1. What state is shaded?

   _____

Math

What time was it 30 minutes ago?

2. _____   3. _____

4. Why should you never iron a four leaf clover?

_____

_____

It's not good to press your luck.

All rights reserved   ECS Learning Systems, Inc.   *Wake Up, Brain!!* • Grade 5

Wake Up, Brain!!

Name: _____

Grammar

1. no one believed copernicus theory that the planets orbit the sun

   _____

   _____

2. the moores youngest daughter is a excellent student

   _____

   _____

Spelling

Write the word that is spelled correctly.

3. corse   course   corsse   _____

4. frunt   frount   front   _____

5. Americen   Americon   American   _____

Language

6. Write the possessive form for each noun.

   school   _____   county   _____

   deer   _____   ocean   _____

   radio   _____   report   _____

          All rights reserved

Wake Up, Brain!!

Name: _____

Geography

1. Which three continents does the Mediterranean Sea border?

   _____   _____

   _____

2. Is Russia north or south of the equator?

   ☐ North   ☐ South

Math

3. Write in standard form.

   Six hundred fifty thousand thirty _____

4. Round these numbers to the nearest hundred.

   5825 _____   6825 _____

   8607 _____

5. Holes fastened to holes, chilly to feel, mostly empty, but strong as steel. What is it?

   _____

   _____

A chain.

All rights reserved   ECS Learning Systems, Inc.   *Wake Up, Brain!!* • Grade 5   9

Wake Up, Brain!!

Name: _____

Grammar

1. conrads father a businessman went on are field trip to the university of idaho

_____

_____

2. her parents who loved life were lots of fun

_____

_____

Spelling

Write the word that is spelled correctly.

3. erly   early   earley   _____

4. I'll   Il'l   Ill'   _____

5. does   dos   des   _____

Language

Add an adjective to make the sentence more descriptive.

6. Julia wants a blouse. _____

7. I sat in my chair. _____

8. The horse went into a field. _____

ECS Learning Systems, Inc.   All rights reserved

Wake Up, Brain!!

Name: _____

Geography

1. What direction is Georgia from Florida?

   ☐ north   ☐ south   ☐ east   ☐ west

2. What continents touch the Pacific Ocean?

   _____

   _____

Math

3. Sunnyside Elementary School has 330 fourth and fifth graders, 250 second graders, and 175 first graders. How many more first and second graders are there than fourth and fifth graders?

   _____

4. $(7 + 9) + 6 = 7 + ($ _____ $+ 6)$

5. Though it's close to your eyes, you'll have to admit
   It's hard to get more than a quick glimpse of it. What is it?

   _____

   Your nose.

All rights reserved   ECS Learning Systems, Inc.   *Wake Up, Brain!!* • Grade 5

Wake Up, Brain!!

Name: _____

Grammar

1. she study education in college and want to be a teacher

   _____

   _____

2. megan want to worked as a nurse at st josephs hospital

   _____

   _____

Spelling

Write the correctly spelled words.

3. roastted   roasted   _____

4. plased   placed   _____

5. dropped   droped   _____

6. turnned   turned   _____

Language

7. Write the past tense of the following verbs.

call		amaze	
study		excite	
wait		clean	
worry		help	

Wake Up, Brain!!

Name: _____

Geography

1. What map symbol identifies direction?

   _____

   _____

2. What kind of map shows landforms?

   _____

   _____

Math

3. How much did the temperature rise from February to May?

   _____

4. What is the temperature difference from January to June?

   _____

Temperature Graph

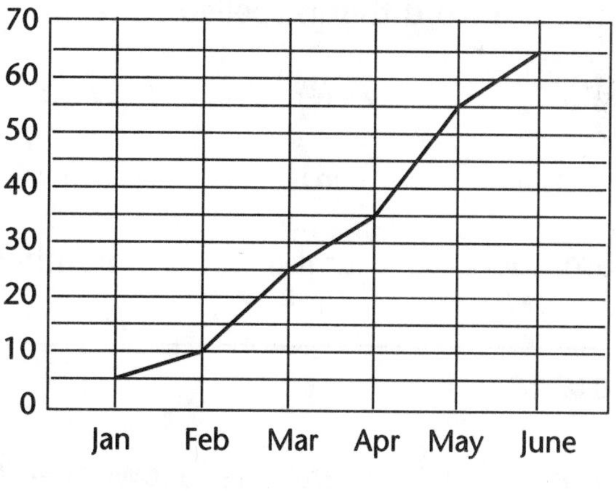

Vertical axis: 0, 10, 20, 30, 40, 50, 60, 70
Horizontal axis: Jan, Feb, Mar, Apr, May, June

5. Some days are rainy, some days are fair. Friday comes before Thursday. Where?

   _____

   _____

In the dictionary.

All rights reserved   ECS Learning Systems, Inc.   *Wake Up, Brain!!* • Grade 5   13

Wake Up, Brain!!

Name: _____

Grammar

1. by fall my book wake up, brain will be done

   _____

   _____

2. before school starts mrs ball needs to write a literature study on the american girl.

   _____

   _____

Spelling

Write the word that is spelled correctly.

3. watar   water   watter   _____

4. words   werds   wordds   _____

5. nummber   numbar   number   _____

Language

6. Write the past tense to the following verbs.

take		know	
eat		go	
face		read	
become		turn	

Wake Up, Brain!!

Name: _____

Geography

1. What kind of maps show boundaries created by people?

   _____

2. What states border the Pacific Ocean?

   _____

   _____

Math

Write the symbol to show whether the first number is **less than** or **greater than** the second number.

3. 463 _____ 482

4. 201 _____ 250

5. 351 _____ 315

6. 898 _____ 989

7. When the bank goes broke, that's not funny. But what kind of bank needs no money?

   _____

   _____

A riverbank.

All rights reserved   ECS Learning Systems, Inc.   *Wake Up, Brain!!* • Grade 5   15

Wake Up, Brain!!

Name: _____

Grammar

1. he gived a speech at the new colonial arts theatre

   _____

   _____

2. the boy catched the baseball in his mit.

   _____

   _____

Spelling

Write the word that is spelled correctly.

3. great   graet   grat   _____

4. oon   oun   own   _____

5. aloung   along   aloung   _____

Language

6. Write the contraction for these words.

I am		they will	
we have		were not	
must not		we shall	
should not		she has	

ECS Learning Systems, Inc.   All rights reserved

Wake Up, Brain!!

Name: _____

Geography

1. What ocean is west of where you live?

   _____

2. What ocean is east of where you live?

   _____

Math

Write the products.

3. 3 x 5 = _____

4. 7 x 2 = _____

5. 5 x 5 = _____

6. 9 x 4 = _____

7. 7 x 4 = _____

8. 4 x 8 = _____

9. Tell me the answer to this if you will. When will water stop running downhill?

   _____

   _____

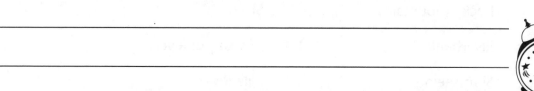

When it gets to the bottom.

All rights reserved   ECS Learning Systems, Inc.   *Wake Up, Brain!!* • Grade 5   17

Wake Up, Brain!!

Name: _____

Grammar

1. if she can found it shell send it to me in south carolina

   _____

   _____

2. jennifer chelsea kim and me has been friends since kindergarten

   _____

   _____

Spelling

Write the word that is spelled correctly.

3. while   wil   whil   _____

4. larg   large   larje   _____

5. often   offen   offten   _____

Language

6. Underline each proper noun.

Ocean	Atlantic
Rocky Mountains	Street
Riverbank	Mississippi River
Sightseeing	Nile River

Wake Up, Brain!!

Name: _____

Geography

1. What is called "the tree plain of Arctic regions?"

   _____

2. What is the landmass called that mainly consists of jungles?

   _____

Math

Using centimeters:

3. How long is this rectangle? _____

   [rectangle box]

4. What is the perimeter of the rectangle? _____

5. If 2's company and 3's a crowd and bees live in a hive,
   tell me now, for crying out loud, what are four and five?

   _____

   _____

Nine.

All rights reserved   ECS Learning Systems, Inc.

Wake Up, Brain!!

Name: _____

Grammar

1. rhinos is the second largest land animal only elephants is bigger

_____

_____

2. a rhino uses a keen sense of smell to protect hisself

_____

_____

Spelling

Write the word that is spelled correctly.

3. togeter   togather   together   _____

4. werld   world   wirld   _____

5. importent   important   impportant   _____

Language

6. What do these abbreviations stand for?

Mr.	
U.S.	
Jr.	
St.	
Dr.	

ECS Learning Systems, Inc.   All rights reserved

Wake Up, Brain!!

Name: _____

Geography

1. Which country is bigger?

   ☐ Mexico   ☐ Italy

2. On what continent is Italy located?

   _____

Math

3. 8 ÷ 2 = _____   4.   16 ÷ 2 = _____

5. 24 ÷ 4 = _____   6.   81 ÷ 9 = _____

7. Troy bought 56 lollipops. The lollipops come in packages of 8. How many packages did he buy?

   _____

8. What never asks any questions at all, yet often is answered by short and tall?

   _____

   _____

The telephone.

All rights reserved   ECS Learning Systems, Inc.   *Wake Up, Brain!!* • Grade 5

Wake Up, Brain!!

Name: _____

Grammar

1. the clown started the day with 128 balloons at the end of the day he only had 18 left

   _____

   _____

2. the highest clouds in the sky called cirrus usually mean fair weather

   _____

   _____

Spelling

Write the words that are spelled correctly.

3. form   formn   forrm   _____

4. liffe   life   lif   _____

5. enough   enouf   enogh   _____

Language

6. Circle **S** next to singular words and **P** next to plural.

mouse	S	P	men	S	P
bush	S	P	Earth	S	P
children	S	P	tribesmen	S	P
cow	S	P	fish	S	P

Wake Up, Brain!!

Name: _____

Geography

In what state would you find:

1. the Space Needle? _____

2. the Alamo? _____

3. the Grand Canyon? _____

Math

4. What fraction of the rectangle is shaded?

   _____

5. Circle the diagram that is NOT a right angle.

6. What has four fingers and a thumb, but neither flesh nor bone,
   Is small or large or medium, but seldom alone.

   _____

   _____

A glove.

All rights reserved   ECS Learning Systems, Inc.   *Wake Up, Brain!!* • Grade 5

Wake Up, Brain!!

Name: _____

Grammar

1. them clouds are puffy and cottony and the shapes is always changing theyre called cumulus

   _____

   _____

2. a book with a title the ghost of blackcrow hill is probably a nonfiction

   _____

   _____

Spelling

Write the words that are spelled correctly.

3.	live	liv	livve	_____
4.	erth	earth	earrth	_____
5.	hihg	highe	high	_____

Language

6. Use an apostrophe to make the bolded nouns possessive.

house of the **men**	
car of the **boy**	
toy of the **child**	
books of the **children**	

     ECS Learning Systems, Inc.   All rights reserved

Wake Up, Brain!!

Name: _____

Geography

1. Name the continent north of South America.

   _____

2. What is the capital of Maine?

   _____

Math

3.   984
     − 320
   _____

4.   6479
     + 42
   _____

5.   10
      x 3
   _____

6.   6 x 3 =   6 x 4 =
     6 x 30 =   6 x 40 =
     6 x 300 =   6 x 400 =
     6 x 3000 =   6 x 4000 =

   What is the pattern?_____

7. Full all day, empty at rest, both of us are very hard-pressed. What are we?

   _____

   _____

A pair of shoes.

All rights reserved

Wake Up, Brain!!

Name: _____

Grammar

1. stratus are low clouds they look like wide gray blankets snow and drizzling rain falls from them

    _____

    _____

2. newspapers and magazines they are called periodicals

    _____

    _____

Spelling

Write the words that are spelled correctly.

3. studey	study	studie	_____
4. second	sekond	seconnd	_____
5. since	sinse	sence	_____

Language

6. Write whether each verb is in the past, present, or future tense.

wants		thought	
learn		cheered	
will help		destroyed	

ECS Learning Systems, Inc.   All rights reserved

Wake Up, Brain!!

Name: _____

Geography

1. Name six countries located in Europe.

_____

_____

_____

_____

Math

2. Finish the pattern.

14   21   28   35   _____   _____   _____   _____

3. 8 x 3 = _____   4. 5 x 9 = _____

5. What island was largest on Earth anywhere,
   Before Australia was known to be there?

_____

_____

Australia.

All rights reserved   ECS Learning Systems, Inc.   *Wake Up, Brain!!* • Grade 5   27

Wake Up, Brain!!

Name: _____

Grammar

1. robins were first called redbreasts because the fronts of there bodies is red

   _____

   _____

2. robins they eat spiders worms insects and small seeds

   _____

   _____

Spelling

   Write the words that are spelled correctly.

3. whiet	whitte	white	_____
4. sentense	setence	sentence	_____
5. across	acrose	acros	_____

Language

6. Write whether each verb is in the past, present, or future tense.

visit		found	
liked		landed	
will dance		excited	

ECS Learning Systems, Inc.   All rights reserved

Wake Up, Brain!!

Name: _____

Geography

1. Name five western states.

_____

_____

_____

_____

_____

Math

2. It's 7:15. What time was it 25 minutes ago?

_____

3. $4 + 7 + 2 + 3 + 6 + 9 =$ _____

4. $72 - 39 =$ _____   5. $87 - 67 =$ _____

6. Little white birds float down through the air
   And light in the trees when they are bare. What is it?

_____

_____

snow.

All rights reserved   ECS Learning Systems, Inc.

Wake Up, Brain!!

Name: _____

Grammar

1. everything around you are called the environment

_____

_____

2. insects have six legs and spiders have eight insects have feelers but spider do not

_____

_____

Spelling

Write the words that are spelled correctly.

3. durring   dureing   during   _____

4. however   houever   howevr   _____

5. shure   sure   surr   _____

Language

6. Write a pronoun for each word.

mayor		students	
sister		forest	
computer		people	

ECS Learning Systems, Inc.   All rights reserved

Wake Up, Brain!!

Name: _____

Geography

1. Name five southern states.

_____

_____

_____

_____

_____

Math

2.
9 ÷ 3 =	72 ÷ 8 =	32 ÷ 8 =
90 ÷ 30 =	720 ÷ 80 =	320 ÷ 80 =
900 ÷ 300 =	7200 ÷ 800 =	3200 ÷ 800 =

What is the pattern? _____

3. What time is it? _____

4. If you crawled into a hole and dug, dug, dug like a mole,
   And like a mole wiggled your snout,
   Where finally would you come out?

_____

_____

Out of the hole.

All rights reserved   ECS Learning Systems, Inc.   *Wake Up, Brain!!* • Grade 5

Wake Up, Brain!!

Name: _____

Grammar

1. the boy's havent gone camping in a long time is they going this summer

   _____

   _____

2. one of americas greatest inventors thomas edison only went to school for three months

   _____

   _____

Spelling

Write the word that is spelled correctly.

3. young   yung   youg   _____

4. heer   hear   haer   _____

5. factory   factery   factry   _____

Language

6. Underline all the letters that should be capitalized.

   bernadette ball

   3530 spring creek road

   idaho falls, idaho, u.s.a.

ECS Learning Systems, Inc.   All rights reserved

Wake Up, Brain!!

Name: _____

Geography

1. Name five midwestern states.

   _____

   _____

   _____

Math

2. 4 x 7 = _____   8 x 7 = _____   4 x 9 = _____

3. 7 x 6 = _____   4 x 6 = _____   10 x 8 = _____

4. 63 ÷ 7 = _____   49 ÷ 7 = _____   81 ÷ 9 = _____

5. 45 ÷ 5 = _____   40 ÷ 4 = _____   72 ÷ 8 = _____

6. What can go through the water and yet
   Not ever become the least bit wet?

   _____

   _____

Sunlight.

All rights reserved   ECS Learning Systems, Inc.   *Wake Up, Brain!!* • Grade 5

Wake Up, Brain!!

Name: _____

Grammar

1. rats mice gophers beavers squirrels and porcupines are all rodents that eat mostly seeds and vegetables

   _____

   _____

2. all rodents have a set of long sharp teeth incisors they use to eat their food

   _____

   _____

Spelling

Write the word that is spelled correctly.

3. example   exampel   exampell   _____

4. hurd   heard   haerd   _____

5. ahaed   ahed   ahead   _____

Language

6. Underline the words that should be capitalized.

   dear mom,

   i hope you will be able to attend jenny's

   graduation. she is excited to be going

   to college at utah state university.

                    love,

                    michelle

ECS Learning Systems, Inc.   All rights reserved

Wake Up, Brain!!

Name: _____

Geography

1. Name five northwestern states.

_____

_____

_____

Math

2. What fraction of the diagram is shaded?

_____

3. It's now 8:30. What time will it be in 3 hours and 40 minutes?

_____

4. When you buy eggs on a farm while out for a ride,
   How can you be sure they have no chickens inside?

_____

_____

Buy duck eggs.

All rights reserved   ECS Learning Systems, Inc.   *Wake Up, Brain!!* • Grade 5   35

Wake Up, Brain!!

Name: _____

Grammar

1. penguins are birds that cant fly but them is excellent swimmers

   _____

   _____

2. pelicans spear fish with its sharp bills and keep there food in a pouch

   _____

   _____

Spelling

Write the word that is spelled correctly.

3. sevral   sveral   several   _____

4. chanje   change   chage   _____

5. bruther   brother   brothre   _____

Language

A possessive pronoun shows ownership. Underline the possessive pronouns.

6. Val likes her stove.

7. Doug likes his job.

8. Carol and Rebecca are excited about their cars.

Wake Up, Brain!!

Name: _____

Geography

1. Name the four southwestern states.

_____

_____

_____

_____

Math

2. Fudgebars come in packages of eight. I need enough for 25 people. How many packages do I need? Show your work.

_____

3.   9 x 2 =   8 x 9 =

    18 ÷ 9 =   72 ÷ 9 =

4. Have you the slightest notion what bus crossed the ocean?

_____

_____

Columbus.

All rights reserved   ECS Learning Systems, Inc.   *Wake Up, Brain!!* • Grade 5

Wake Up, Brain!!

Name: _____

Grammar

1. volleyball is a team sport wear players hit a ball over the net

   _____

   _____

2. players they can use there heads or there hands to hit the ball

   _____

   _____

Spelling

Write the words that are spelled correctly.

3. answer   anser   anwser   _____

4. agaisnt   agenst   against   _____

5. turnned   turned   terned   _____

Language

6. Write four compound words.

7. What is the meaning of the word "proceed"?

   _____

Wake Up, Brain!!

Name: _____

Geography

1. On what continent are the Canadian Rockies?

   _____

2. On what continent is Argentina?

   _____

Math

3. Complete the boxes.

Favorite	
Least Favorite	

   Favorite Fruit

   (bar graph: Pear = 15, Apple = 25, Peach = 20, Plum = 10; y-axis 0 to 25)

4. Peaches have _____ more votes than pears.

5. Guess this for me if you can: how long should be the legs of a man?

   _____

   _____

Long enough to reach the ground.

All rights reserved   ECS Learning Systems, Inc.   *Wake Up, Brain!!* • Grade 5   39

Wake Up, Brain!!

Name: _____

Grammar

1. the mostest famous of all the rocky mountains is pikes peak

_____

_____

2. the whether is colder at the top of most mountains

_____

_____

Spelling

Write the words that are spelled correctly.

3. learn   lern   larn   _____

4. poynt   poent   point   _____

5. towerd   toward   towrad   _____

Language

6. Write an adjective for each noun.

NOUN	ADJECTIVE
Venus	
Earth	
stars	

ECS Learning Systems, Inc.   All rights reserved

Wake Up, Brain!!

Name: _____

Geography

1. What part of a map shows distance?

   _____

2. What countries does Mexico border?

   _____

Math

3. Draw a line of symmetry in each shape.

4. I tell folks their faults, though I can't make a sound.
   Even so, they must like me cuz they keep me around. What am I?

   _____

   _____

A mirror.

All rights reserved   ECS Learning Systems, Inc.   *Wake Up, Brain!!* • Grade 5

Wake Up, Brain!!

Name: _____

Grammar

1. the pueblo native americans have lived in new mexico and arizona. four hundreds of years

   _____

   _____

2. the pueblos dances were peaceful they danced when they asked the gods for rain or sunshine

   _____

   _____

Spelling

Write the words that are spelled correctly.

3. usualy   usually   usaully   _____

4. monye   monie   money   _____

5. morning   merning   mornning   _____

Language

6. Write verbs that are more precise.

eat	
play	
talk	
take	

Wake Up, Brain!!

Name: _____

Geography

1. The Arctic Ocean passes through what continents?

   _____

2. What is the capital city of Hawaii?

   _____

Math

3. Circle the figures that have $\frac{1}{2}$ turn symmetry.

4. Use words to write these numbers.

   400,000 _____

   98,000 _____

5. What wears clothes in the summertime when it's too hot to scold,
   But none at all in the winter when winds are blowing cold?

   _____

   _____

A tree.

All rights reserved ECS Learning Systems, Inc. *Wake Up, Brain!!* • Grade 5   43

Wake Up, Brain!!

Name: _____

Grammar

1. robots they are controlled by computers and do many useful jobs that people find boring

   _____

   _____

2. flying airplanes and building cars are some of the jobs perfom by robots

   _____

   _____

Spelling

Write the words that are spelled correctly.

3. familey   fammily   family   _____

4. grup   group   groop   _____

5. treu   true   troo   _____

Language

6. An adjective describes a noun. Write an adjective for each noun.

ocean	
car	
dance	
planet	

ECS Learning Systems, Inc.   All rights reserved

Wake Up, Brain!!

Name: _____

Geography

1. Name the four hemispheres of the world.

    _____ and _____

    _____ and _____

2. What is the longest river in the world?

    _____

Math

3. Shade the circles to show $\frac{3}{4}$.

    ◯ ◯ ◯

4. One yard = _____ inches

5. One mile = _____ feet

6. If now you miss this riddle, perhaps you'll guess it later:
    What is it that stays hot longest in the refrigerator?

    _____

    _____

A pepper.

All rights reserved   ECS Learning Systems, Inc.   *Wake Up, Brain!!* • Grade 5   45

Wake Up, Brain!!

Name: _____

Grammar

1. some sheeps grow 20 pounds of fleece each year cutting off the fleece are called shearing

   _____

   _____

2. after the fleece is cut off it is call wool witch is used to make clothing

   _____

   _____

Spelling

Write the words that are spelled correctly.

3. haff   halv   half   _____

4. United States   United State   Untied States _____

5. order   orrder   ordar   _____

Language

6. Write a synonym for each word.

sparkling	
evening	
dark	
hot	

ECS Learning Systems, Inc.   All rights reserved

Wake Up, Brain!!

Name: _____

Geography

1. Name a state that is a peninsula.

   _____

   _____

2. How is a peninsula different from an island?

   _____

   _____

Math

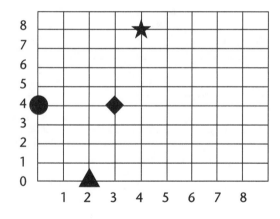

3. What figure appears at:

   0,4 _____

   4,8 _____

   3,4 _____

   2,0 _____

4. Full of beats, wears a cowhide cap,
   And never speaks till you give it a slap. What is it?

   _____

   _____

A drum.

All rights reserved   ECS Learning Systems, Inc.   *Wake Up, Brain!!* • Grade 5

Wake Up, Brain!!

Name: _____

Grammar

1. have you ever smelled a skunk the smell it comes from scent glands under its tail

   _____

   _____

2. to protect himself, skunks arch his backs and shoot the smelly liquid 10 feet into the air

   _____

   _____

Spelling

Write the words that are spelled correctly.

3. bulevard   boulavard   boulevard   _____

4. frount   frunt   front   _____

5. Americen   American   Ammerican   _____

Language

6. Write an antonym for each word.

chilly	
difficult	
bright	
loud	

Wake Up, Brain!!

Name: _____

Geography

1. Name the hemisphere that has more water.

   _____

2. Name the Great Lake that is only in the U.S.

   _____

Math

3.
12	21	37
x 7	x 6	x 3

4.
268	802	4792
+ 339	− 569	+ 895

5. Big enough to hold a pig, small enough to be held like a twig. What is it?

   _____

   _____

A pen.

All rights reserved   ECS Learning Systems, Inc.   *Wake Up, Brain!!* • Grade 5

Wake Up, Brain!!

Name: _____

Grammar

1. an author names parson weems wrote a book about george washington

   _____

   _____

2. mr weems made up the story about young george washington chopping down the cherry tree

   _____

   _____

Spelling

Write the words that are spelled correctly.

3. eerly   erly   early   _____

4. I'll   Il'l   I'l   _____

5. deos   does   des   _____

Language

6. Write a homonym for each word.

heard	
weight	
they're	
great	

ECS Learning Systems, Inc.   All rights reserved

Wake Up, Brain!!

Name: _____

Geography

1. Name a famous bay between Maryland and Virginia.

   _____

2. Name the three continents the Tropic of Cancer passes through.

   _____

Math

3. Michelle ran around the perimeter of the block below. How far did she run? _____

4. $8\overline{)24}$

5. $6\overline{)42}$

6. $36 \div 9 =$ _____

7. $81 \div 9 =$ _____

200 yards

50 yards

50 yards

200 yards

8. Which weighs more, when all has been said,
   A pound of feathers or a pound of lead?

   _____

   _____

They weigh the same.

All rights reserved   ECS Learning Systems, Inc.   *Wake Up, Brain!!* • Grade 5

Wake Up, Brain!!

Name: _____

Grammar

1. people plants and animals are living things in you're environment

   _____

   _____

2. air water and soil are non-living things finded in you're environment

   _____

   _____

Spelling

Write the words that are spelled correctly.

3. brout   broght   brought   _____

4. closse   close   clos   _____

5. though   thogh   thugh   _____

Language

Write whether each statement is fact or opinion.

6. George Washington was President. _____

7. The U.S. is the best country. _____

8. Everyone celebrates July 4th. _____

9. The 4th of July is a national holiday. _____

ECS Learning Systems, Inc.   All rights reserved

Wake Up, Brain!!

Name: _____

Geography

1. What capital city of one of the 50 United States is on an island?

   _____

2. Name the continents the Atlantic Ocean touches.

   _____

Math

3.
   $$5,467$$
   $$+ \ 6,755$$

   $$470,292$$
   $$+ \ 82,467$$

4. Patrick's team had 42 players. There were 7 bats. How many kids would have to share a bat?

   _____

5. Round as a wheel, hollow as a cup.
   Forty thousand elephants couldn't pull it up. What is it?

   _____

   _____

A well.

All rights reserved   ECS Learning Systems, Inc.   *Wake Up, Brain!!* • Grade 5

Wake Up, Brain!!

Name: _____

Grammar

1. there are several consonants and consonant blends that make the K sound they are c k ch ck and qu

   _____

   _____

2. most sentences must have to things: a noun and a verb

   _____

   _____

Spelling

Write the words that are spelled correctly.

3. idea   ideea   ide   _____

4. befor   befour   before   _____

5. becam   becaem   became   _____

Language

"Negative" means NO. Two negative words should never be together.

6. Underline the sentence that has a double negative.

   He would not never go to the movie alone.

   He would never go to the movie alone.

54   *Wake Up, Brain!!* • Grade 5   ECS Learning Systems, Inc.   All rights reserved

Wake Up, Brain!!

Name: _____

Geography

1. Name 10 states east of the Mississippi River.

Math

2. Allison found 82,426 rocks. Susan found 46,892. How many more did Allison find than Susan?

_____

3.   48   82   65
     x 8   x 5   x 6
    _____   _____   _____

4. What can you hold, no matter how old, in your left hand
   That you can't hold, no matter how bold, in your right hand?

   _____

   _____

Your right elbow.

All rights reserved   ECS Learning Systems, Inc.   *Wake Up, Brain!!* • Grade 5

Wake Up, Brain!!

Name: _____

Grammar

1. people they use oceans in many ways but the waters has to be protected from pollution

   _____

   _____

2. when industries and factories use oceans as dumping grounds for waste water plants and animals are harmed

   _____

   _____

Spelling

Write the words that are spelled correctly.

3. behinnd   behend   behind   _____

4. canot   cannot   canott   _____

5. amung   among   amuong   _____

Language

A suffix changes the meaning of a word. Suffix examples:
er, ist, or, ness, ment, ful, less, ous, ly, able, ing, en.

6. Add suffixes to these words.

wide	care
use	hunt
power	chill

ECS Learning Systems, Inc.   All rights reserved

Wake Up, Brain!!

Name: _____

Geography

1. Name 10 states west of the Mississippi River.

Math

2.

321	124	312
x 6	x 2	x 4

3. 1 ten-dollar bill, 3 five-dollar bills, 2 one-dollar bills, 1 quarter, 2 nickels, 1 penny

    How much money is this? _____

4. I really don't mean to give you a scare, but when is a boy most like a bear?

    _____

    _____

When he is barefoot.

All rights reserved   ECS Learning Systems, Inc.

Wake Up, Brain!!

Name: _____

Grammar

1. rachel carson wrote the sea around us under the sea-wind and the edge of the sea

   _____

   _____

2. ms carson loved the ocean even though she was 22 years old before she seed it for the first time

   _____

   _____

Spelling

Write the words that are spelled correctly.

3. liquid   liqiud   licquid   _____

4. contry   cuontry   country   _____

5. exampel   example   exampal   _____

Language

6. Add a suffix to each word.

thought	enjoy
danger	trick
kind	cheek
beauty	quick

ECS Learning Systems, Inc.   All rights reserved

Wake Up, Brain!!

Name: _____

Geography

1. What country in Europe did the pilgrims come from?

   _____

2. What countries border France in Europe?

   _____

   _____

Math

3.   398   802   872
        x 7   x 7   x 6
      _____   _____   _____

4. Is $10.00 enough to buy three items that cost $3.35 each?

   _____

5. Three birds sat on a fence taking in the air.
   Now what is the difference between here and there?

   _____

   _____

The letter "t".

All rights reserved   ECS Learning Systems, Inc.   *Wake Up, Brain!!* • Grade 5

Wake Up, Brain!!

Name: _____

Grammar

1. do you have a nickname nicknames are silly names people call each other

   _____

   _____

2. most people dont mind if there friends make up a nice nickname

   _____

   _____

Spelling

Write the words that are spelled correctly.

3. thesarus   thesaurus   thesarous   _____

4. heros   hereos   heroes   _____

5. should   shuold   shulde   _____

Language

6. Write six present-tense verbs.

Wake Up, Brain!!

Name: _____

Geography

1. Name the states that border the Gulf of Mexico.

   _____

   _____

   _____

   _____

Math

2. Jane has $867.52 in her checking account. She is writing a check for $182.56. How much will she have left in her checking account?

   _____

3.
   701   109   702
   x 9   x 8   x 3
   _____   _____   _____

4. It has 88 keys and needs no more, but can't unlock a single door. What is it?

   _____

   _____

A piano.

All rights reserved   ECS Learning Systems, Inc.   *Wake Up, Brain!!* • Grade 5   61

Wake Up, Brain!!

Name: _____

Grammar

1. scientist jonas salk invented a vaccine that wood prevent polio whats a vaccine

   _____

   _____

2. in a way we are all scientists we are always trying to find answers to things we dont understand

   _____

   _____

Spelling

Write the words that are spelled correctly.

3. different   diffirent   diferent   _____

4. perhapps   peraps   perhaps   _____

5. sertain   certain   sertan   _____

Language

6. Write six subjects of a sentence.

   ECS Learning Systems, Inc.   All rights reserved

Wake Up, Brain!!

Name: _____

Geography

1. What sea does most of the London coastline border?

   _____

   _____

2. Which is most mountainous in the United States—the east or the west?

   _____

Math

Polygons are closed shapes formed by straight lines.

3. Draw a polygon with four equal sides. What is it?

   _____

4. Draw a polygon with five equal sides. What is it?

   _____

5. Draw a polygon with six equal sides. What is it?

   _____

6. Why do you suppose it would be all wrong
   If your pretty nose were twelve inches long?

   _____

   _____

The "it" would be a "foot"!

All rights reserved   ECS Learning Systems, Inc.   *Wake Up, Brain!!* • Grade 5

Wake Up, Brain!!

Name: _____

Grammar

1. sometimes indoor air is know safer than outside air because air pollution is indoors two

   _____

   _____

2. indoor pollution can cause sickness and disease people need too help make the indoor environment safe

   _____

   _____

Spelling

Write the words that are spelled correctly.

3. redy   ready   reddy   _____

4. bilt   builtt   built   _____

5. spechel   speial   special   _____

Language

6. Write two declarative sentences.

   _____

   _____

   _____

   _____

ECS Learning Systems, Inc.   All rights reserved

Wake Up, Brain!!

Name: _____

Geography

1. The Caribbean Sea and the Pacific Ocean are connected by what famous canal?

   _____

2. What lake is full of salt and located in Utah?

   _____

Math

3. D.D. Mudd's Restaurant served 1,126 dinners for seven days in a row. How many dinners did they serve all together?

   _____

4.
3,862	3,016	2,000
x 3	x 6	x 9

5. Can't walk but runs very well. Can't talk but makes people yell. What is it?

   _____

   _____

A taxicab.

All rights reserved

ECS Learning Systems, Inc.

Wake Up, Brain!!

Name: _____

Grammar

1. when something is biodegradable it means it will eventually fall a part and become part of the soil

   _____

   _____

2. when we take things out of the earth that we cant put back it is harmful to the environment

   _____

   _____

Spelling

Write the words that are spelled correctly.

3. compleet   complete   complet   _____

4. hundred   hunderd   hunerd   _____

5. thosand   thuosand   thousand   _____

Language

6. Write two interrogative sentences.

   _____

   _____

   _____

   _____

ECS Learning Systems, Inc.   All rights reserved

Wake Up, Brain!!

Name: _____

Geography

1. What is the capital of Brazil?

   _____

2. What country borders Argentina in the west?

   _____

Math

3.
7.17	0.25	29.50
x 5	x 4	x 5

4. What time will it be in an hour and a quarter?

   _____

5. Though not a soldier, I often fight. Though not a musician, I sing before light. Though not a clock, I wake people up. What am I, then, if I'm not a pup?

   _____

   _____

A rooster.

All rights reserved   ECS Learning Systems, Inc.   *Wake Up, Brain!!* • Grade 5

Wake Up, Brain!!

Name: _____

Grammar

1. the king didnt want robin hood to be a hero he was a thief

   _____

   _____

2. robin hood stole from the rich king and gave to the poor he outsmarted the kings men every time

   _____

   _____

Spelling

Write the words that are spelled correctly.

3. keppt   kept   keptt   _____

4. notise   notice   nottice   _____

5. voyce   voice   voise   _____

Language

6. Write two exclamatory sentences.

   _____

   _____

   _____

   _____

ECS Learning Systems, Inc.   All rights reserved

Wake Up, Brain!!

Name: _____

Geography

1. What is the only continent that is a country and an island?

   _____

2. Which is smaller, Europe or Asia?

   _____

Math

3. Draw a figure, divide it into fourths, and shade one half.

4. Draw a figure, divide it into thirds, and shade one third.

5. What can't walk a step, but matter of factly
   Possesses a hundred legs exactly?

   _____

   _____

Fifty pairs of pants.

All rights reserved ECS Learning Systems, Inc. *Wake Up, Brain!!* • Grade 5

Wake Up, Brain!!

Name: _____

Grammar

1. leif eriksson was a viking who found america long before christopher columbus

_____

_____

2. starting in norway eriksson sailed across the atlantic ocean and landed near the us and canadian border

_____

_____

Spelling

Write the words that are spelled correctly.

3. probbly   probaly   probably   _____

4. area   areea   arrea   _____

5. rownd   rownde   round   _____

Language

6. Write two complete sentences. Underline the verbs and circle the complete subjects.

_____

_____

_____

_____

ECS Learning Systems, Inc.   All rights reserved

Wake Up, Brain!!

Name: _____

Geography

1. What is the name of the small islands southeast of Australia?

   _____

2. What is the capital of North Carolina?

   _____

Math

3.
$$\begin{array}{r} \$18.02 \\ \times\ 7 \\ \hline \end{array} \qquad\qquad \begin{array}{r} 5482 \\ \times\ 6 \\ \hline \end{array}$$

$$\begin{array}{r} 8,685 \\ \times\ 3 \\ \hline \end{array} \qquad\qquad \begin{array}{r} \$30.10 \\ \times\ 4 \\ \hline \end{array}$$

4. If you had to give your things away and didn't know what to start with, What single item would you say is the easiest thing to part with?

   _____

   _____

A comb.

All rights reserved   ECS Learning Systems, Inc.   *Wake Up, Brain!!* • Grade 5

Wake Up, Brain!!

Name: _____

Grammar

1. antonia novello was the first female and the first hispanic united states surgeon general

   _____

   _____

2. surgeon general antonia said i know that if i make good sense people might be willing to make good changes

   _____

   _____

Spelling

Write the words that are spelled correctly.

3. usully   usuelly   usually   _____

4. relly   really   realy   _____

5. remember   rememmber   rembor   _____

Language

6. Write six common nouns.

     ECS Learning Systems, Inc.   All rights reserved

Wake Up, Brain!!

Name: _____

Geography

1. Name three continents the Arctic Ocean touches.

   _____

   _____

2. Name the states surrounding Kentucky.

   _____

   _____

Math

3. $3\overline{)81}$ $9\overline{)279}$

      $6\overline{)126}$ $7\overline{)287}$

4. What time will it be in six hours?

   _____

5. If you bounce a green pea off a bass drum
   And into the sea, what will be become?

   _____

   _____

Wet.

All rights reserved   ECS Learning Systems, Inc.   *Wake Up, Brain!!* • Grade 5

Wake Up, Brain!!

Name: _____

Grammar

1. sum flowers stay closed unless the light is bright

   _____

   _____

2. one flower the midday flower changes colors its yellow when it blooms and changes to pink to days later

   _____

   _____

Spelling

Write the words that are spelled correctly.

3. corse   cours   course   _____

4. brought   broght   borught   _____

5. happenned   happened   hapened   _____

Language

6. Rewrite these nouns in their possessive form.

mother	
nurses	
dogs	
parrot	

Wake Up, Brain!!

Name: _____

Geography

1. What river passes through the Grand Canyon?

   _____

2. What is the largest country in South America?

   _____

Math

3. The brick weighed 160 pounds. It broke into eight equal pieces. How much did each piece weigh?

   _____

4. $192 \div 32 =$ _____

5. $128 \div 32 =$ _____

6. Tell me what nut, when nails are gone, you might hang a picture on.

   _____

   _____

A "Wall" nut.

All rights reserved   ECS Learning Systems, Inc.   *Wake Up, Brain!!* • Grade 5

Wake Up, Brain!!

Name: _____

Grammar

1. a post card is a way too send a short message two a friend

   _____

   _____

2. you write the address on the write side of the card and you're message on the left

   _____

   _____

Spelling

Write the words that are spelled correctly.

3. befor   beafor   before   _____

4. English   Enlish   Englesh   _____

5. paece   peice   piece   _____

Language

6. Write six pronouns.

ECS Learning Systems, Inc.   All rights reserved

Wake Up, Brain!!

Name: _____

Geography

1. Which is the smallest ocean?

   _____

2. What direction would you travel from North Dakota to Oklahoma?

   _____

Math

3. 1 gallon = _____ quarts

4. ½ gallon = _____ quarts

5. 1 liter is **about** the same as a   ❐ pint   ❐ quart   ❐ gallon

6. 1 liter = 1,000 milliliters. What does 2 liters equal?

   _____

7. You know the moon is like a cheese, but what nut is like a sneeze?

   _____

A cashew nut.

All rights reserved   ECS Learning Systems, Inc.   *Wake Up, Brain!!* • Grade 5

Wake Up, Brain!!

Name: _____

Grammar

1. we went to the carnival and rided the bumper cars

   _____

   _____

2. ben joe and phil they went on the roller coaster 14 times

   _____

   _____

Spelling

Write the words that are spelled correctly.

3. yere   year   yeer   _____

4. coontry   countrey   country   _____

5. picher   picture   piture   _____

Language

Make the following phrases in possessive form using an apostrophe.

6. A pencil belonging to Julie _____

7. A moon of the Earth _____

8. The mayor of New York _____

9. A space shuttle of Cape Canaveral _____

Wake Up, Brain!!

Name: _____

Geography

1. On what continent is China located?

   _____

2. Where does the Mississippi River start?

   _____

Math

3. Circle the shapes that have four right angles.

   □   △   ▭

4. 416 + 135 + 27 + 43 + 6 = _____

5. What goes "99, Clunk, 99, Clunk, 99, Clunk?"

   _____

   _____

A centipede with a wooden leg.

All rights reserved   ECS Learning Systems, Inc.

Wake Up, Brain!!

Name: _____

Grammar

1. many student are in the honor society and studys very hard

   _____

   _____

2. mrs bird the history teacher travels to europe every year

   _____

   _____

Spelling

Write the words that are spelled correctly.

3. eech   each   eche   _____

4. thees   theas   these   _____

5. bene   been   baen   _____

Language

A helping verb works with the main verb. Underline the helping verb in each sentence.

6. The carpenters are building a house.

7. The rain is pouring down.

8. We are sitting down.

9. We have measured the blocks.

          All rights reserved

Wake Up, Brain!!

Name: _____

Geography

1. Where is the Golden Gate Bridge?

   _____

2. What group of islands is one of the United States?

   _____

Math

One hundred children voted for their favorite ice cream.

3. How many voted for chocolate?

   _____

Favorite Ice Cream

4. How many voted for vanilla?

   _____

5. What flavor received the least votes?

   _____

Banana–10—
Strawberry–15—
— Chocolate–50
Vanilla–25—

6. How do you avoid ticks on your pets?

   _____

   _____

Don't let them wear a watch.

All rights reserved   ECS Learning Systems, Inc.   *Wake Up, Brain!!* • Grade 5   81

Wake Up, Brain!!

Name: _____

Grammar

1. alaska canada and greenland was on the cruise were taking

_____

_____

2. saturns ring contains crystals and gases

_____

_____

Spelling

Write the words that are spelled correctly.

3. ground   grownd   grond   _____

4. realy   really   relly   _____

5. remember   remmember   remembar   _____

Language

An adverb modifies a verb, adjective, or another adverb. Underline the adverbs.

6. The car moved swiftly.

7. The beans totally filled the jar.

8. The class was completely silent.

Wake Up, Brain!!

Name: _____

Geography

1. What is the capital city of Idaho? _____

2. Name 3 gulfs by the United States.

   _____

   _____

   _____

Math

More than or greater than? Write the correct symbol.

3. 423 ◯ 482

4. 202 ◯ 220

5. 262 ◯ 226

6. 434 ◯ 432

7. Write the words for 4,802. _____

8. How does a farmer count his cows?

   _____

   _____

With a "cow-culator."

All rights reserved   ECS Learning Systems, Inc.   *Wake Up, Brain!!* • Grade 5

Wake Up, Brain!!

Name: _____

Grammar

1. polar bears is excellent swimmers

   _____

   _____

2. i are sure polar bears love the cold said karen

   _____

   _____

Spelling

Write the words that are spelled correctly.

3. understad   understand   understannd   _____

4. animel   animal   annimal   _____

5. power   pouer   powre   _____

Language

6. Write five abbreviations and their meanings.

Wake Up, Brain!!

Name: _____

Geography

1. What famous river begins in Cairo, Egypt?

   _____

2. What sea is by Cairo, Egypt?

   _____

Math

3.
88	53	849
x 4	x 6	x 7

4. To what number is the arrow pointing?

   _____

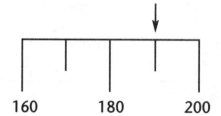

160   180   200

---

5. Why did the astronaut skip class?

   _____

   _____

It was launch time.

All rights reserved   ECS Learning Systems, Inc.   *Wake Up, Brain!!* • Grade 5

Wake Up, Brain!!

Name: _____

Grammar

1. michelle will you help clean up this mess

   _____

   _____

2. no I need to work on my homework that mrs jensen gave us

   _____

   _____

Spelling

Write the words that are spelled correctly.

3. hevey   heavy   heavvy   _____

4. carfully   carefully   carrfully   _____

5. folow   fullow   follow   _____

Language

6. Write four plural words and their singular form.

ECS Learning Systems, Inc.   All rights reserved

Wake Up, Brain!!

Name: _____

Geography

1. What state below has the warmest climate?

   ☐ Idaho   ☐ Florida   ☐ Maine

2. Name a continent the equator runs through.

   _____

Math

3. $8\overline{)712}$ $3\overline{)183}$ $7\overline{)420}$

4. $\dfrac{1}{12} + \dfrac{2}{3} =$ _____

5. $\dfrac{2}{8} + \dfrac{1}{2} =$ _____

6. $\dfrac{3}{10} + \dfrac{3}{5} =$ _____

7. This you may answer perhaps in a hurry,
    When is a blackberry not a blackberry?

    _____

    _____

When it is green (or red).

All rights reserved   ECS Learning Systems, Inc.   *Wake Up, Brain!!* • Grade 5

Wake Up, Brain!!

Name: _____

Grammar

1. ronnie the new boy in school is from australia

   _____

   _____

2. my favorite foods are pizza bananas and chocolate

   _____

   _____

Spelling

Write the words that are spelled correctly.

3. everywon   everyone   evvreyone   _____

4. leve   leave   leeve   _____

5. system   sistem   systemm   _____

Language

6. Write the abbreviations for the first six months of a year.

ECS Learning Systems, Inc.   All rights reserved

Wake Up, Brain!!

Name: _____

Geography

1. To travel from Seattle, Washington, to Los Angeles, California, what direction would you go?

   _____

2. What famous mountain range is found in India?

   _____

Math

3. Thirty-four kids will play soccer on two teams of 11 each. The remaining players will be alternates. How many alternates will each team have?

   _____

4. Draw hands on this clock to show 11:47.

5. Be so kind as to answer me: What nut do you find on the shore of the sea?

   _____

   _____

A beach nut.

All rights reserved   ECS Learning Systems, Inc.   *Wake Up, Brain!!* • Grade 5

Wake Up, Brain!!

Name: _____

Grammar

1. we appreciated mr. carr fixing the sole of my shoe

_____

_____

2. luckily john was not in much pane when he fell

_____

_____

Spelling

Write the words that are spelled correctly.

3. wach   watch   wache   _____

4. within   witthen   wethen   _____

5. themsels   themselfs   themselves   _____

6. begen   begin   beggin   _____

Language

7. Write six pairs of synonyms.

ECS Learning Systems, Inc.   All rights reserved

Wake Up, Brain!!

Name: _____

Geography

1. What two states are outside the contiguous U.S.?

   _____   _____

   _____   _____

2. What continent does the Arctic Circle pass through?

   _____

Math

3. Write these numbers in decimal form.

   $\frac{9}{10}$ _____ $49\frac{4}{10}$ _____

   $19\frac{17}{100}$ _____ $5\frac{8}{10}$ _____

4. $82\overline{)1230}$ $77\overline{)231}$

5. Of all things weak or strong, in lightness it is first,
   But if you try to hold it long, you feel that you will burst. What is it?

   _____

   _____

Your breath.

All rights reserved   ECS Learning Systems, Inc.   *Wake Up, Brain!!* • Grade 5

Wake Up, Brain!!

Name: _____

Grammar

1. the hartwell corp provides great service said a representative from firemans fund company

   _____

   _____

2. pluto our farthest planet is a great mystery

   _____

   _____

Spelling

Write the words that are spelled correctly.

3. therd   third   thierd   _____

4. quite   quitte   queit   _____

5. carryed   careed   carried   _____

Language

6. Write four pair of antonyms.

ECS Learning Systems, Inc.   All rights reserved

Wake Up, Brain!!

Name: _____

Geography

1. Which continent surrounds the South Pole?

   _____

2. What is the capital city of Maryland?

   _____

Math

3.
   9344   2096   878
   x 24   x 16   x 24
   _____   _____   _____

4. Circle the right angles.

5. Railroad crossing! Look out for the cars! Can you spell that without any Rs?

   _____

   _____

T-H-A-T

All rights reserved   ECS Learning Systems, Inc.

Wake Up, Brain!!

Name: _____

Grammar

1. mrs belnap sure are funny and i like she's jokes

   _____

   _____

2. is the cars rebecca and conrad got green and black

   _____

   _____

Spelling

Write the words that are spelled correctly.

3. distance   distence   distanse   _____

4. paralell   parallel   parralled   _____

5. verble   verble   verbal   _____

Language

6. Write four pairs of homonyms.

Wake Up, Brain!!

Name: _____

Geography

1. What is a physical map?

_____

_____

_____

_____

Math

2. $15\overline{)525}$ $48\overline{)672}$ $98\overline{)686}$

3. What fraction of each rectangle is shaded?

_____   _____

4. What crosses the land from coast to coast, but continues to stand as still as a post?

_____

_____

The highway.

All rights reserved   ECS Learning Systems, Inc.

Wake Up, Brain!!

Name: _____

Grammar

1. these womens clothes were made by a famous fashion designer from paris france

   _____

   _____

2. she belongs to the young readers club

   _____

   _____

Spelling

Write the words that are spelled correctly.

3. possibel   posibble   possible   _____

4. together   togethor   twogether   _____

5. dosn't   does'nt   doesn't   _____

Language

6. Write four verbs and their past tense form.

ECS Learning Systems, Inc.   All rights reserved

Wake Up, Brain!!

Name: _____

Geography

1. What is a political map?

_____

_____

_____

_____

Math

2.

$$\frac{3}{3} = \frac{}{12}$$ $$\frac{3}{5} = \frac{}{10}$$

$$\frac{2}{4} = \frac{}{12}$$ $$\frac{1}{4} = \frac{}{12}$$

$$\frac{5}{5} = \frac{}{10}$$ $$\frac{1}{5} = \frac{}{20}$$

3. Are you able to guess what can fill a whole house
   And still weigh less than a tiny mouse?

_____

_____

smoke.

All rights reserved   ECS Learning Systems, Inc.   *Wake Up, Brain!!* • Grade 5   97

Wake Up, Brain!!

Name: _____

Grammar

1. in washington dc we went to the air and space museum

   _____

   _____

2. mrs johnsons house was a very victorian design

   _____

   _____

Spelling

Write the words that are spelled correctly.

3. beuty   beutey   beauty   _____

4. picksure   picture   pichter   _____

5. cabnet   cabinit   cabinet   _____

Language

6. Write eight contractions.

Wake Up, Brain!!

Name: _____

Geography

1. What state has the smallest land area?

   _____

   _____ •

2. What state has the largest land area?

   _____

   _____

Math

3. What is $\frac{1}{4}$ of 32? _____

4. What is $\frac{1}{8}$ of 8? _____

5. What is $\frac{1}{3}$ of 27? _____

---

6. What travels faster than creatures with toes, but touches nothing as it goes?

   _____

   _____

Your voice.

All rights reserved   ECS Learning Systems, Inc.   *Wake Up, Brain!!* • Grade 5   99

Wake Up, Brain!!

Name: _____

Grammar

1. the equator the tropic of capricorn and the tropic of cancer all pass through africa

   _____

   _____

2. did you no the pacific ocean touches all continents except europe and africa

   _____

   _____

Spelling

Write the words that are spelled correctly.

3. famly   famley   family   _____

4. tardy   tardey   tarrdy   _____

5. cafeterea   cafeteria   cafateria   _____

Language

6. A declarative sentence states an idea. Write two declarative sentences.

   _____

   _____

ECS Learning Systems, Inc.   All rights reserved

Wake Up, Brain!!

Name: _____

Geography

1. Name the oceans that touch North America.

   _____

   _____

2. What is the capital city of Montana?

   _____

Math

3. Write these fractions in order from least to greatest.

   $\frac{4}{8}$, $\frac{8}{8}$, $\frac{3}{8}$ _____

   $\frac{1}{2}$, $\frac{3}{4}$, $\frac{1}{4}$ _____

   $\frac{3}{10}$, $\frac{4}{10}$, $\frac{1}{2}$ _____

4. I'm sometimes strong and sometimes weak, but I am nobody's fool.
   For there is no language I can't speak, though I never went to school. What am I?

   _____

   _____

An echo.

All rights reserved   ECS Learning Systems, Inc.   *Wake Up, Brain!!* • Grade 5

Wake Up, Brain!!

Name: _____

Grammar

1. that idea was mine said bethany i thought of it first?

    _____

    _____

2. hers article the first computer is rather unusual

    _____

    _____

Spelling

Write the words that are spelled correctly.

3. readdy   ready   redy   _____

4. guidde   guide   giude   _____

5. sister   sisster   sistar   _____

Language

6. An interrogative sentence asks a question. Write two interrogative sentences.

    _____

    _____

    _____

    ECS Learning Systems, Inc.   All rights reserved

Wake Up, Brain!!

Name: _____

Geography

1. What great mountain range is in the western United States?

   _____

2. What great mountain range is in the eastern United States?

   _____

Math

3. 9 x 9 = _____   9 x 6 = _____   11 x 5 = _____

4. 9 x 7 = _____   8 x 6 = _____   5 x 9 = _____

5. Round to the nearest 100.

   5,876 _____   9,408 _____

6. What has panes but doesn't ache, is very hard, but easy to break?

   _____

   _____

A window.

All rights reserved   ECS Learning Systems, Inc.   *Wake Up, Brain!!* • Grade 5   103

Wake Up, Brain!!

Name: _____

Grammar

1. john glenn once an astronaut are now a senator

   _____

   _____

2. dr mclain cares a great deal about his patients hes an excellent doctor

   _____

   _____

Spelling

Write the words that are spelled correctly.

3. tomorow   tamorrow   tomorrow   _____

4. vidio   video   vedio   _____

5. koaster   caoster   coaster   _____

Language

6. Write the present tense form of each verb.

fought	
known	
ran	
gave	

ECS Learning Systems, Inc.   All rights reserved

Wake Up, Brain!!

Name: _____

Geography

1. The smallest ocean in the world is:

   _____

2. Topeka is the capital city of what state?

   _____

Math

3. Show the measurement in centimeters.

your desktop	
your shoe	
your pointer finger	
your ruler	

4. Three ladies heard it thunder. Three ladies all got under one small umbrella (or tried to get). Why didn't the three ladies get wet?

   _____

   _____

It didn't rain.

All rights reserved   ECS Learning Systems, Inc.   *Wake Up, Brain!!* • Grade 5

Answer Key

Note: Grammar activities may occasionally have more than one possible answer.

Page 6
1. Would you be surprised if I didn't talk for two hours?
2. Karen asked you to call her before 7:30. Did you?
3. be, house, know, little, ride, stop
4. 2, 4, 1, 3

Page 7
1. Oklahoma
2. 1:00
3. 3:00

Page 8
1. No one believed Copernicus' theory that the planets orbit the sun.
2. The Moore's youngest daughter is an excellent student.
3. course
4. front
5. American
6. school's, county's, deer's, ocean's, radio's, report's

Page 9
1. Africa, Europe, Asia
2. North
3. 650,030
4. 5,800; 6,800; 8,600

Page 10
1. Conrad's father, a businessman, went on our field trip to the University of Idaho.
2. Her parents, who loved life, were lots of fun.
3. early
4. I'll
5. does
6. Example: Julia wants a green blouse.
7. Example: I sat in my favorite chair.
8. Example: The horse went into an empty field.

Page 11
1. North
2. Russia, Australia, North America, South America
3. 95
4. 9

Page 12
1. She studies education in college and wants to be a teacher.
2. Megan wants to work as a nurse at St. Joseph's Hospital.
3. roasted
4. placed
5. dropped
6. turned
7. called, amazed, studied, excited, waited, cleaned, worried, helped

Page 13
1. compass rose
2. A physical map
3. 45 degrees
4. 60 degrees

Page 14
1. By fall my book, Wake Up, Brain!!, will be done.
2. Before school starts, Mrs. Ball needs to write a literature study on The American Girl.
3. water
4. words
5. number
6. took, knew, ate, gone, faced, read, became, turned

Page 15
1. political maps
2. Alaska, California, Hawaii, Washington, Oregon
3. <
4. <
5. >
6. <

Page 16
1. He gave a speech at the new Colonial Arts Theater.
2. The boy caught the baseball in his mitt.
3. great
4. own
5. along
6. I'm, they'll, we've, weren't, mustn't, we'll, shouldn't, she's

Page 17
1. Pacific Ocean (with the exception of students in Alaska and Hawaii.)
2. Atlantic Ocean (with the exception of students in Alaska and Hawaii.)
3. 15
4. 14

5. 25
6. 36
7. 28
8. 32

Page 18
1. If she can find it she'll send it to me in South Carolina.
2. Jennifer, Chelsea, Kim, and I have been friends since kindergarten.
3. while
4. large
5. often
6. Atlantic, Rocky Mountains, Mississippi River, Nile River

Page 19
1. Tundra
2. Rain forest
3. 8 cm
4. 18 cm

Page 20
1. Rhinos are the second largest land animal. Only elephants are bigger.
2. A rhino uses a keen sense of smell to protect himself.
3. together
4. world
5. important
6. Mister, United States, Junior, Street or Saint, Doctor or Drive

Page 21
1. Mexico
2. Europe
3. 4
4. 8
5. 6
6. 9
7. 7 packages

Page 22
1. The clown started the day with 128 balloons. At the end of the day he only had 18 left.
2. The highest clouds in the sky, called cirrus, usually mean fair weather.
3. from
4. life
5. enough
6. Mouse-S, men-P, bush-S, Earth-S, Children-P, tribesmen-P, cow-S, fish-S & P

ECS Learning Systems, Inc.   All rights reserved

Answer Key

Page 23
1. Washington
2. Texas
3. Arizona
4. One third
5. The center diagram is NOT a right angle.

Page 24
1. Those clouds are puffy and cottony and the shapes are always changing. They're called "cumulus."
2. A book with a title <u>The Ghost of Blackcrow Hill</u> is probably a nonfiction.
3. live
4. earth
5. high
6. men's house, boy's car, child's toy, children's books

Page 25
1. North America
2. Augusta
3. 664
4. 6,521
5. 30
6. Multiples of 10

Page 26
1. Stratus are low clouds. They look like wide, gray blankets. Snow and drizzling rain falls from them.
2. Newspapers and magazines are called "periodicals."
3. study
4. second
5. since
6. Wants-present, thought-past, learn-present or future, cheered-past, will help- future, destroyed-past

Page 27
1. Answers will vary but must contain six countries within Europe.
2. 42, 49, 56, 63
3. 24
4. 45

Page 28
1. Robins were first called "redbreasts" because the fronts of their bodies are red.

2. Robins eat spiders, worms, insects, and small seeds.
3. white
4. sentence
5. across
6. Visit-present or future, found-past, liked-past, landed-past, will dance-future, excited-present.

Page 29
1. Answers will vary but must contain appropriate western states.
2. 6:50
3. 31
4. 33
5. 20

Page 30
1. Everything around you is called the environment.
2. Insects have six legs and spiders have eight. Insects have feelers but spiders do not.
3. during
4. however
5. sure
6. Mayor-her, she, his, hers, or him, students-them, they, we, sister-her, forest-it, computer-it, people-them, they, we

Page 31
1. Answers will vary but must contain appropriate southern states.
2. Multiples of 10
3. 9:55

Page 32
1. The boys haven't gone camping in a long time. Are they going this summer?
2. One of America's greatest inventors, Thomas Edison, only went to school for three months.
3. young
4. hear
5. factory
6. <u>B</u>ernadette <u>B</u>all
   3530 <u>S</u>pring <u>C</u>reek <u>R</u>oad
   <u>I</u>daho <u>F</u>alls, <u>I</u>daho, <u>U.S.A</u>.

Page 33
1. Answers will vary but must contain appropriate Midwestern states.
2. 28, 56, 36
3. 42, 24, 80
4. 9, 7, 9
5. 9, 10, 9

Page 34
1. Rats, mice, gophers, beavers, squirrels, and porcupines are all rodents that eat mostly seeds and vegetables.
2. All rodents have a set of long, sharp teeth, incisors, they use to eat their food.
3. example
4. heard
5. ahead
6. <u>D</u>ear, <u>M</u>om, <u>I</u>, <u>J</u>enny's, <u>S</u>he, <u>U</u>tah <u>S</u>tate <u>U</u>niversity, <u>L</u>ove, <u>M</u>ichelle

Page 35
1. Answers will vary but must contain appropriate northwestern states.
2. 2/6 or 1/3
3. 12:10

Page 36
1. Penguins are birds that can't fly, but they are excellent swimmers.
2. Pelicans spear fish with their sharp bills and keep their food in a pouch.
3. several
4. change
5. brother
6. her
7. his
8. their

Page 37
1. Answers will vary but must contain appropriate southwest states.
2. 4 packages (25 ÷ 8 = 3.1)
3. 18, 72, 2, 8

Page 38
1. Volleyball is a team sport where players hit a ball over the net.
2. Players can use their heads or their hands to hit the ball.
3. answer
4. against

All rights reserved ECS Learning Systems, Inc. *Wake Up, Brain!!* • Grade 5

Answer Key

5. turned
6. Answers will vary but must be accepted compound words.
7. To go on or go ahead

Page 39
1. North America
2. South America
3. Apple, Plum
4. 5

Page 40
1. The most famous of all the Rocky Mountains is Pike's Peak.
2. The weather is colder at the top of most mountains.
3. learn
4. point
5. toward
6. Answers will vary but should contain an adjective that adequately describes each noun.

Page 41
1. The scale
2. Guatemala and the U.S.
3. Each shape should have a line drawn through it that divides the shape in equal halves.

Page 42
1. The Pueblo Native Americans have lived in New Mexico and Arizona for hundreds of years.
2. The Pueblos' dances were peaceful. They danced when they asked the gods for rain or sunshine.
3. usually
4. money
5. morning
6. Answers will vary but should contain a descriptive replacement for the verbs.

Page 43
1. North America, Europe, Asia
2. Honolulu
3. Square, circle, octagon
4. Four hundred thousand Ninety-eight thousand

Page 44
1. Robots are controlled by computers and do many useful jobs that people find boring.
2. Flying airplanes and building cars are some of the jobs performed by robots.
3. family
4. group
5. true
6. Answers will vary but should contain an adjective that adequately describes each noun.

Page 45
1. north and south, east and west
2. Nile
3. 3/4 of each circle should be shaded.
4. 36
5. 5,280

Page 46
1. Some sheep grow 20 pounds of fleece each year. Cutting off the fleece is called "shearing."
2. After the fleece is cut off it is called "wool" which is used to make clothing.
3. half
4. United States
5. order
6. Answers will vary but must include a synonym for each word.

Page 47
1. Florida
2. An island is surrounded on all sides by water.
3. ●, ★, ◆, ▲

Page 48
1. Have you ever smelled a skunk? The smell comes from scent glands under its tail.
2. To protect himself, a skunk arches its back and shoots the smelly liquid 10 feet into the air.
3. boulevard
4. front
5. American
6. Answers will vary but must include an antonym for each word.

Page 49
1. western
2. Lake Michigan
3. 84, 126, 111
4. 607, 233, 5,687

Page 50
1. An author named Parson Weems wrote a book about George Washington.
2. Mr. Weems made up the story about young George Washington chopping down the cherry tree.
3. early
4. I'll
5. does
6. Answers may vary but must include an homonym for each word.

Page 51
1. Chesapeake Bay
2. North America, Africa, Asia
3. 500 yards
4. 3
5. 7
6. 4
7. 9

Page 52
1. People, plants, and animals are living things in your environment.
2. Air, water, and soil are non-living things found in your environment.
3. brought
4. close
5. though
6. fact
7. Opinion
8. Opinion
9. Fact

Page 53
1. Honolulu
2. North America, South America, Europe, Asia, Antarctica
3. 12,222; 552,759
4. 6

Page 54
1. There are several consonants and consonant blends that make the K sound. They are c, k, ch, ck, and qu.
2. Most sentences have two things: a noun and a verb.
3. idea
4. before
5. became
6. He would not never go to the movie alone.

ECS Learning Systems, Inc.   All rights reserved

Answer Key

Page 55
1. MS, AL, GA, FL, SC, NC, VA, WV, IL, IN, OH, PA, NY, MD, DE, NJ, CT, RI, MA, NH, VT
2. 35,534
3. 384, 410, 390

Page 56
1. People use oceans in many ways, but the waters have to be protected from pollution.
2. When industries and factories use oceans as dumping grounds for waste, plants, and animals are harmed.
3. behind
4. cannot
5. among
6. Answers will vary.

Page 57
1. WA, OR, CA, NV, AZ, UT, ID, MT, WY, CO, MN, TX, OK, KS, NE, SD, ND, MN, IA, MO, AR, LA, AK, HI
2. 1926, 248, 1248
3. $27.36

Page 58
1. Rachel Carson wrote <u>The Sea Around Us</u>, <u>Under the Sea-wind</u>, and <u>The Edge of the Sea</u>.
2. Ms. Carson loved the ocean even though she was 22 years old before she saw it for the first time.
3. liquid
4. country
5. example
6. Answers will vary but an appropriate suffix should be added to each word.

Page 59
1. England
2. Switzerland, Italy, Germany, Belgium, Spain
3. 2786, 5614, 5232
4. No (Total = $10.05)

Page 60
1. Do you have a nickname? Nicknames are silly names people call each other.
2. Most people don't mind if their friends make up a nice nickname.
3. thesaurus
4. heroes
5. should

6. Examples: do, come, hear, are, is

Page 61
1. TX, LA, MS, AL, FL
2. $684.96
3. 6309, 872, 2106

Page 62
1. Scientist Jonas Salk invented a vaccine that would prevent polio. What's a vaccine?
2. In a way, we are all scientists. We are always trying to find answers to things we don't understand.
3. different
4. perhaps
5. certain
6. Answers will vary but must include words that would indicate a sentence subject.

Page 63
1. North Sea
2. the west
3. square
4. pentagon
5. hexagon

Page 64
1. Sometimes indoor air is no safer than outside air because air pollution is indoors, too.
2. Indoor pollution can cause sickness and disease. People need to help make the indoor environment safe.
3. ready
4. built
5. special
6. Answers must include two declarative sentences.

Page 65
1. Panama Canal
2. Salt Lake
3. 7,882
4. 11,586; 18,096; 18,000

Page 66
1. When something is biodegradable, it means it will eventually fall apart and become part of the soil.

2. When we take things out of the earth that we can't put back, it is harmful to the environment.
3. complete
4. hundred
5. thousand
6. Answers must include two interrogative sentences.

Page 67
1. Brasilia
2. Chile
3. 35.85; 1; 147.50
4. 8:45

Page 68
1. The king didn't want Robin Hood to be a hero. He was a thief.
2. Robin Hood stole from the rich king and gave to the poor. He outsmarted the king's men every time.
3. kept
4. notice
5. voice
6. Answers must include two exclamatory sentences.

Page 69
1. Australia
2. Europe
3. A figure must be drawn and divided into 4ths.
4. A figure must be drawn and divided into 3rds.

Page 70
1. Leif Eriksson was a Viking who found America long before Christopher Columbus.
2. Starting in Norway, Eriksson sailed across the Atlantic Ocean and landed near the U.S. and Canadian border.
3. probably
4. area
5. round
6. Answers will vary but must contain two complete sentences with verbs underlined and complete subjects circled.

Page 71
1. New Zealand
2. Raleigh
3. $126.14; 32,892; 26,055; $120.40

All rights reserved   ECS Learning Systems, Inc.   *Wake Up, Brain!!* • Grade 5

Answer Key

Page 72
1. Antonia Novello was the first female and the first Hispanic United States Surgeon General.
2. Surgeon General Antonia said, "I know that if I make good sense, people might be willing to make good changes."
3. usually
4. really
5. remember
6. Answers must include six common nouns.

Page 73
1. Asia, Europe, North America
2. TN, VA, WV, OH, IN, IL, MO
3. 27, 31, 21, 41
4. 7:30

Page 74
1. Some flowers stay closed unless the light is bright.
2. One flower, the midday flower, changes colors. It's yellow when it blooms and changes to pink two days later.
3. course
4. brought
5. happened
6. Mother's, nurses', dogs', parrot's

Page 75
1. Colorado River
2. Brazil
3. 20 pounds
4. 6
5. 4

Page 76
1. A post card is a way to send a short message to a friend.
2. You write the address on the right side of the card and your message on the left.
3. before
4. English
5. piece
6. Answers must contain six pronouns.

Page 77
1. Arctic
2. south
3. 4
4. 2
5. Quart

6. 2,000 ml

Page 78
1. We went to the carnival and rode the bumper cars.
2. Ben, Joe, and Phil went on the roller coaster 14 times!
3. year
4. country
5. picture
6. Julie's pencil
7. The Earth's moon
8. New York's major
9. Cape Canaveral's space shuttle

Page 79
1. Asia
2. Lake Itasca, Minneapolis
3. Square, rectangle
4. 627

Page 80
1. Many students are in the Honor Society and study very hard.
2. Mrs. Bird, the history teacher, travels to Europe every year.
3. each
4. these
5. been
6. are
7. is
8. are
9. have

Page 81
1. San Francisco, CA
2. Hawaii
3. 50
4. 25
5. Banana

Page 82
1. Alaska, Canada, and Greenland are on the cruise we're taking.
2. Saturn's ring contains crystals and gases.
3. ground
4. really
5. remember
6. swiftly
7. totally
8. completely

Page 83
1. Boise
2. Gulf of Mexico, Gulf of Alaska, Gulf of California
3. <
4. <
5. >
6. >
7. Four thousand eight hundred two

Page 84
1. Polar bears are excellent swimmers.
2. "I am sure polar bears love the cold," said Karen.
3. understand
4. animal
5. power
6. Answers must include five words and their correct abbreviation.

Page 85
1. Nile River
2. Mediterranean Sea
3. 352, 318, 5943
4. 190

Page 86
1. Michelle, will you help clean up this mess?
2. No, I need to work on my homework that Mrs. Jensen gave us.
3. heavy
4. carefully
5. follow
6. Answers must include four words and their proper plural form.

Page 87
1. Florida
2. South America
3. 89, 61, 60
4. 9/12 or 3/4
5. 6/8 or 3/4
6. 9/10

Page 88
1. Ronnie, the new boy in school, is from Australia.
2. My favorite foods are pizza, bananas, and chocolate.
3. everyone
4. leave
5. system
6. Jan., Feb., Mar., Apr., May, Jun.

ECS Learning Systems, Inc. All rights reserved

Answer Key

Page 89
1. South
2. Himalayas
3. 6
4. Clock hands should show 11:47.

Page 90
1. We appreciated Mr. Carr fixing the sole of my shoe.
2. Luckily, John was not in much pain when he fell.
3. watch
4. within
5. themselves
6. begin
7. Answers will vary but must include four pair of appropriate synonyms.

Page 91
1. Hawaii, Alaska
2. Greenland
3. .9; 49.4; 19.17; 5.8
4. 15, 3

Page 92
1. "The Hartwell Corp. provides great service," said a representative from Fireman's Fund Company.
2. Pluto, our farthest planet, is a great mystery.
3. third
4. quite
5. carried
6. Answers will vary but must include four pair of appropriate antonyms.

Page 93
1. Antarctica
2. Annapolis
3. 224,256; 33,536; 21,072
4. The second and fourth figures contain right angles.

Page 94
1. Mrs. Belnap sure is funny and I like her jokes.
2. Are the cars Rebecca and Conrad got green and black?
3. distance
4. parallel
5. verbal
6. Answers will vary but must include four pair of appropriate homonyms.

Page 95
1. Physical maps show features such as borders and topography.
2. 35, 14, 7
3. 1/4, 2/3

Page 96
1. These women's clothes were made by a famous designer from Paris, France.
2. She belongs to the Young Readers' Club.
3. possible
4. together
5. doesn't
6. Answers will vary but must include four verbs and their appropriate past tense.

Page 97
1. A political map shows the highest concentration of political parties in an area.
2. 12/12; 6/10, 6/12, 3/12, 10/10, 4/20

Page 98
1. In Washington, D.C., we went to the Air and Space Museum.
2. Mrs. Johnson's house was a very Victorian design.
3. beauty
4. picture
5. cabinet
6. Answers will vary but must include eight appropriate contractions.

Page 99
1. Rhode Island
2. Alaska
3. 8
4. 1
5. 9

Page 100
1. The equator, the Tropic of Capricorn, and the Tropic of Cancer all pass through Africa.
2. Did you know the Pacific Ocean touches all continents except Europe and Africa?
3. family
4. tardy
5. cafeteria

6. Answers will vary but must include two correctly-written declarative sentences.

Page 101
1. Atlantic, Arctic, Pacific
2. Helena
3. 3/8, 4/8, 8/8
   1/4, 1/2, 3/4
   3/10, 4/10, 1/2

Page 102
1. "That idea was mine," said Bethany, "I thought of it first."
2. Her topic, "The First Computer," is rather unusual.
3. ready
4. guide
5. sister
6. Answers will vary but must include two correctly-written interrogative sentences.

Page 103
1. Rocky Mountains
2. Appalachian Mountains
3. 81, 54, 55
4. 63, 48, 45
5. 5900, 9400

Page 104
1. John Glenn, once an astronaut, is now a senator.
2. Dr. McLain cares a great deal about his patients. He's an excellent doctor.
3. tomorrow
4. video
5. coaster
6. fight, know, run, give

Page 105
1. Antarctic
2. Kansas
3. Answers will vary but must be stated in appropriate centimeters.

All rights reserved

ECS Learning Systems, Inc.

About the Authors

After graduating from the University of Utah, **Michelle Ball** (right) lived in Salt Lake City before returning to her hometown of Idaho Falls, Idaho. She has three children, Conrad, Rebecca, and Patrick. Her husband, Doug, is a great support in her life and has always valued her love for teaching. He is an active part of her school life and known in the neighborhood as "Mrs. Ball's Husband."

Michelle's 15 years of teaching experiences in kindergarten, second, and third grades provided a sound foundation for her current position as a teacher in a multi-age classroom. "Teaching three grades at once has definitely enhanced my life (my dear friend and co-author's daughter was my student). Working in a multi-age classroom has provided opportunities to develop organizational skills and teaching strategies that benefit my students. Working with children has given me countless joys. My students have enriched my life beyond measure."

Barbara Morris (left) grew up and received her education in Idaho. A career in banking took her to Utah and California before she and her husband, Tony, became parents and moved back "home" to Idaho to raise their only child, Jennifer. As a new parent, "Barb" developed her own publishing skills and eventually built a small, in-home desktop publishing business.

Barb met Michelle as she enrolled Jennifer in Michelle's multi-grade classroom. Eventually, their relationship developed into a bond of friendship that enhanced both lives and fulfilled their individual goals and dreams. As a full-time office manager for a local hospital, Barb had little time to volunteer in the classroom, but had a desire to stay involved with her child's education. She offered her desktop publishing skills to Michelle, who sketched out student worksheets, literature studies, and classroom management tools. Barb converted them into the original student-friendly and teacher-helpful *Wake Up, Brain!!*, which developed into the new series for grades 1 through 6.

ECS Learning Systems, Inc. All rights reserved